FROM

A Practical Guide for Starting a Small Business

ASHCO PUBLICATIONS, INC.

ISBN   0-9661937-6-8

To Tricia –

Printed in the United States of America

Thanks –
Gurri

FIRST EDITION

ASHCO PUBLICATIONS, INC.
P.O. BOX 3066
Ashtabula, OH 44005-3066

INTRODUCTION

As you will see, I have tried to portray my experiences, give hints and tips, and add humor so we can both laugh at my mistakes. However, since my business is flowers and gift baskets, this book is a little "slanted" towards that. But don't stop reading—there is still a lot of practical advice that could help even the "worm grower" (which I used to be).

Even though my business is run out of my home, I have included tips for the business that is larger than mine and not run from the home.

My hope is that we have a few laughs together while you are reading and after you have finished this book you will have gained knowledge from my mistakes.

DEDICATIONS

- To Dr. John, my spouse of 40 years. His **spirit, stamina, determination,** sense of **humor,** and **support** got me where I am today. (I think that's good?!)

  I know that sometimes he thinks I have finally gone off the deep end, but he always has the "**spirit**" to go along. His "**stamina**" as he hikes in the cemeteries to find the graves—no matter the weather, and his "**determination**" to pick, hang, and spray the <u>best</u> wildflowers is inspirational.

  The "**humor**" we share is exceptional, as we discuss his hanging-out in the weeds and people waving to him as he is knee-deep in cat tails or getting frost bite in the graveyard.

  Most important of all is the "**support**" he has always given me. I say thank you.

ACKNOWLEDGEMENTS

- A special thank you to Edward A. Stein, my husband's business partner and friend. His financial assistance and encouragement to complete this book was inspiring.

- To Joshua and Jenna, my grandchildren, who are always "in awe" of Grandma's flower room.

TABLE OF CONTENTS

CHAPTER 1

FOR OPENERS

NOW IS THE TIME?....Are you tired of giving all your "creations" away? Does everyone expect you to do it "for free?" Have you made lots of items but have little for yourself? Or do you fit the "always doing something for nothing" model, like painting, cooking, babysitting, pet or house sitting?

If you answered yes to any of these questions, then you <u>should</u> continue to read this book and maybe I can, from some of my past experiences, give you some ideas and hints for starting your own business and turning your talents and efforts into cash.

Even though I complain about giving things away, I certainly have saved a ton of money by using my talents for wedding gifts, funeral baskets, birthdays, births, etc. It took me a while to convince myself that if I am truly in business then why shouldn't I use my products for gifts? Selling a "service" may take a little thought, but I am sure there is a way to give your time and or service as a gift.

When I am asked if I can make this or that—if I think they want a freebee—I ask, "How much do you want to spend?" That puts everyone on the "same page" and nothing is taken for granted.

I must admit though, I am a "softy" when my children ask me to create something for their homes. The praise I get is worth the time and effort—and what the heck—they are my kids!

WHY AND WHAT... Starting any kind of business takes motivation and talent! Take the time to list your reasons for wanting to start your own business—the most common—wanting to make money, be your own boss, develop your talents, and have freedom. However, if you are running away from the grind of going to work everyday and answering to someone else, then you had better give it some more thought because...

<u>you will be your own worst enemy, your own
worst critic, and your own worst slave driver</u>.
If you are truly motivated to make your
business work, you will put more hours a week
into it than you ever thought possible. If you
still want to do this, then…read on.

Decide what you want to do. Let yourself be
flexible, don't marry a single idea —see which
ones work best for you and consider what you
truly enjoy. There is a list of "innovative"
businesses that might interest you at the end of
this book.

You must have the desire, talent and
ambition, or you would not have picked up this
book to read—*So, let's get started!*

BE IN THE KNOW… The first and most
important thing you need to be successful in
your own business is <u>knowledge</u>.

According to research conducted by Dun &
Bradstreet, 90% of all small business failures
can be traced to poor management resulting
from <u>lack of knowledge</u>.

3

This is not a big deal! Knowledge is only as far away as your library or computer. The Internet is available in most libraries, if you haven't purchased a computer yet.

Borrow books from the library and then purchase the ones that will help your business.

If you are still afraid that you don't have enough knowledge about how to manage your business, check the local adult education classes, community colleges, and vocational schools. They frequently run classes that may be exactly what you need and give you the confidence to begin. The good thing is they are usually inexpensive.

My first business was raising worms—I was a worm farmer! Boy did I have a lot to learn, considering I had never even picked up a worm before—and by the way, they are not slimy.

There was very little information about worms in the library—25 years ago—and no Internet. Scientists and farmers had just begun to realize how important worms were to the environment and how our pesticides were killing them off.

I was lucky to find a book written by an elderly couple who had a worm farm. That book became my Bible, and the rest was "trial and error." And believe me—it was truly trial and error—more later.

MAKING MONEY—THE NAME OF THE GAME! Don't let anyone tell you that you are wasting your time. Many people have turned their hobbies into money-making businesses. Who would have thought baking cookies would be big business? People laughed at Debbie Fields—now Mrs. Fields is laughing all the way to the bank.

Why <u>not</u> enjoy what you do for a living? What is more important as we go through life than to have pleasure and enjoyment—if anything just to relieve the everyday stress, or the everyday boredom—whichever is driving you crazy.

Whatever your talents—needlework, sewing, ceramics, painting, pottery, flowers, and so on—you have the know-how and <u>can</u> reap financial benefits.

If your ideas are not arts and crafts it doesn't matter. There are markets for all good ideas, dog sitting, house sitting, window washing, etc. Maybe some of my hints can help. (Remember the worm farm!)

No idea is a bad idea. It is only a bad idea if we don't learn anything from it.

The craft industry is BIG business and there is money to be made! Just take a look at all the new craft supply stores that are around. Millions of people are buying from these stores—they can't be keeping it all for themselves or everyone would have to live in a 150-room mansion! AH! They must have found a way to sell their creations.

The service industry is also BIG business and can be very lucrative. People are purchasing more and more services than ever before. No one wants to spend their free time doing mundane chores. People are living longer and may need help doing chores they used to do or maybe they figure that "life's too short"—let someone else clean my house. More women are entering the workforce and discovering the word "Super Woman" is interchangeable with the word "Stupid Woman."

The bottom line is—today's world is full of opportunities—find a need, fill it, and become profitable.

I know of a lady (obviously an excellent cook) who started a business cooking for people in their homes. She does the shopping, and prepares the meals (for several days.) And the best part is, because the cooking is done in people's homes it eliminates the hassle of dealing with the Health Department and purchasing other licenses relating to preparation of food. Her clientele is made up of professional people as well as the elderly. Imagine coming home from work and your meals are already prepared—just microwave!

And you didn't even have to shop for the groceries.

I saw a car the other day that had a sign on it which read "Sue's Helping Hand." Later I found out that she was a person who was always helping elderly people—neighbors and friends and then decided to start a small business. She runs her business out of her home (no expensive office) and does grocery shopping, runs errands, shuttles people to doctor appointments, as well as some light house cleaning.

Another couple I know started a pet sitting business which later they marketed with a home protection package—what if your hot water tank breaks, what if your refrigerator or freezer stops running, what if the power goes off, or worse yet—a fire? It's a good concept.

They added picking up the mail, checking the house for any problems while the owners are gone, and providing the necessities (milk, bread, etc.) for them upon their return. The ideas are endless.

CHAPTER 2

STARTING UP

WHAT'S IN A NAME? Until the last twenty years it was pretty safe to just look in the yellow pages of your telephone book and see if the name you picked was already taken—no longer!

The Internet has changed that way of thinking. There are millions of web sites for companies all over the world. Research your name thoroughly so you cannot be accused of infringement of someone else's trademark.

After you pick a name it probably would be a good idea to register it as <u>your</u> trademark (check page 16 of this chapter.)

A very good thing to remember when you are considering a name for your business—if you get bored or tired of your creations or service and want to expand to another, your business name should be generic enough to allow you to do it.

I started out thinking I wanted to do gift baskets—and chose the name, "Communicate With Baskets." Sounded good—at least I thought so—then came my children's weddings. After making the bouquets and all the floral decorations I found I enjoyed working with silk flowers more than baskets, but didn't want to totally rule out the baskets—so I changed my name to "Floral and Basket Expressions."

I know you are thinking—SO WHAT! But if you have already printed business cards, paid for a vendor's license, stationery, advertised in the yellow pages, and printed signs, changing your name can be expensive. So give it some thought—although I thought I had "given it some thought."

The worm business was much simpler—first of all no one in my city was raising worms and there was nothing I could expand to except potting soil (which is worm waste)—so the name "Top Hat Worm Farm" worked fine. I designed my logo around a worm with a top hat, cane, vest, and bow tie. It got people's attention and that was what I wanted.

I got a real chuckle every time I was introduced to someone new—they immediately looked down at my hands I guess they thought a worm farmer should have dirty finger nails. I sure had a great time telling people about the business. The question I kept getting over and over was, "Why do you want to raise worms?"

CUTE?

BUSINESS CARDS... Once you have decided on a name, it is a good idea to have business cards printed. Here's another thing I thought I had covered!! I ordered 1,000 very fancy colored business cards (grandiose, I know) and after I had used only about 100 of them—the area code in my town changed. Now I probably could have wall-papered my shop with these cards or changed the area code with a pen (that looked tacky), but decided it was best to throw them away and take the loss. So don't order too many to start—just in case you have to change something—one exception to this tip—sometimes the difference between 500 and 1,000 cards is only a few dollars—go for the best bargain.

If you have a computer you can create your own business cards for practically nothing except for purchasing heavier weight card stock. If you don't have the equipment or just don't want to be bothered—places like Office Max will do business cards very inexpensively. Sometimes it is a good idea to go to a local business person who either prints cards or sells them. Getting to know other owners of small businesses is a wise thing—it can also create business for you and they could become very good friends.

```
                                    Your Name
                                       Title
          Business Name
             (123) 456-7890
                  Slogan

    Address                     fbe@apk.net
    City, State Zip
              Hours By Appointment
              www.floralexpressions.com
```

Don't forget to include your e-mail address
and web site address, if you have one. Give a
card to everyone you meet and put one in every
letter, statement and invoice.

***STATIONERY AND ENVELOPES*...** All of
these can be created on a computer. If you
have a colored printer you can establish a color
scheme for your business tying together all
correspondence and business cards.

CHECKING ACCOUNT... You can use your own personal checking account to start, but it does look a lot more professional to have business checks printed. Besides your friends and relatives (usually our worst critics) will be impressed and begin to really believe you have a business.

Some banks and credit unions offer free checking. Shop around for the best deal. Order checks through the mail—ordering through a bank or credit union is much more costly although you may have to purchase the first set through them.

CREDIT CARDS... Apply for a credit card with no annual fee and a fixed interest rate. If you already have more than one credit card— you can use one of those for business only. It doesn't have to have your business name on it, but having a separate checking account and credit card will keep your business expenses and income separate from your personal use.

14

Keeping your business and personal affairs separated will make doing taxes a lot easier.

*LICENSES...*It may seem unbelievable that your small business would have to comply with numerous local, state, and federal regulations. Most regulations vary by industry—for example, if your business is a food service, you will have to deal with the Department of Health.

Occupying a new or used building requires you to apply for a Certificate of Occupancy from the zoning department.

If you are selling to the "end" buyer or user, you must have a sales tax number and collect sales tax.

Not all states have the same regulations for licenses. It is best to call the local court house and they will put you in the right direction for obtaining licenses necessary for your business or visit http://www.sba.gov/world/states.html.

A sales tax number will be your ticket to multiple savings, as many craft suppliers will give vendor's a discount <u>and</u> you will not pay sales tax on items purchased. Also, many wholesale suppliers will <u>only</u> sell to vendors.

PROTECTION...There are different ways to protect your ideas or creations. Visit http://www.uspto.gov.

<u>Trademarks</u> are names or symbols used in commerce that are regulated by state governments or the U.S. Congress. They are usually good for 10 years. Visit. http://www.sba.gov/world/states.html.

<u>Copyrights</u> protect the rights of authors, musical composers and artists. Visit http://lcweb.loc.gov/copyright.

BOOK KEEPING... If you can add and subtract, you can set up your initial set of books. Ask advice or help from someone who deals with small businesses—not a CPA that works for large corporations—they think too big! At the start up of your business you will have plenty of time to keep you own books since you will still be "learning." That does not mean you need to do the taxes. It is a good idea to go to a professional who specializes in small businesses. Ask other people who own a small business who they use to do their taxes.

STATEMENTS AND INVOICES... If you are smart, you won't spend a lot of money on office supplies. The easiest way to handle this office expense is to purchase a computer and learn to use it. You can save a lot of money by printing your own statements and invoices. Make a master form and use it over and over. Color coordinate with your stationery, statements, invoices and business cards.

STATEMENT

BUSINESS NAME
ADDRESS

PHONE NUMBER   *FAX NUMBER*
E-MAIL ADDRESS   *WEB SITE ADDRESS*

Customer Name_____Date_____
Date of Event _____

Quantity	Description	Unit Price	Amount
		Total	
		Tax	
		Grand Total	

THANK YOU FOR YOUR BUSINESS !

BUSINESS NAME
ADDRESS
PHONE NUMBER
E-MAIL ADDRESS   WEB SITE ADDRESS

<u>stationery</u>

LOOKING GOOD...Always look your best! You and your business have to look successful or people will not believe you are really "the place to go." Paint, clean, straighten up your place of business. Make it look professional.

Dress stylish and make sure your clothes are appropriate, clean and pressed. Drive the best vehicle you can afford and KEEP IT CLEAN— especially if you have advertisement on your car.

Would you want to hire a person to clean or cook for you when they are driving a dirty vehicle?

ATTITUDE ...Don't complain—always say you are "terrific" and business "couldn't be better!" Not only will your customers believe it, you will begin to believe it too! And here comes the positive attitude it takes to get through the rough times!

One of the most important things I feel I have learned from my business is to laugh at my mistakes (and learn). "Cry and you cry alone, laugh and the world laughs with you!"

FAMILY AND FRIENDS… Having a great attitude about your business is very important, but if your <u>only</u> activity is business, your family and friends will suffer. Keep your spouse informed about your business activities, but don't make it your only topic of discussion.

Keep your hobbies alive and get some physical exercise to help you reduce tension and keep your mind clear.

You will be putting in long hours with your new business, but remember to set aside regular time for family and friends—or you may not have family and friends after a while.

INSURANCE… Shop around for insurance for your business. Talk to at least three or four independent agents and compare prices and coverage. In some cities the Chamber of Commerce will offer a group rate for insurance.

Liability Insurance is extremely important as it provides protection for injury or damage to others while on your property. Your personal liability insurance may not cover a business related incident, especially if you are conducting business out of your home.

Disability Insurance will give you an income if you cannot work.

Fire Insurance is mandatory whether you're working out of your home or a separate facility. Discuss a comprehensive policy so that your losses from being out of business are covered also as well as the contents of your business.

Business Interruption Insurance will protect you against loss of revenue because of property damage.

Credit Insurance will pay for losses because of nonpayment of accounts receivable.

Burglary/Robbery/Theft Insurance will cover losses caused by robbery even by your own employees.

Rent Insurance will pay for the rent of another facility if you cannot operate from your normal location.

Worker's Compensation Insurance is necessary if you have employees. Work closely with your insurance agent to make sure you classify your employees correctly for the lowest rate.

If you are working out of your home, your home owners policy may not cover your business. If so, have the insurance agent add a home office rider.

Check your automobile insurance to make sure it covers for business use of your vehicle.

WHAT KIND OF BUSINESS?...You need to decide what type of operation you want. The simplest business structure is called a **sole proprietorship**. It simply means that you are the only owner and you and your business are the same. You become personally liable for all debts of the business.

Partnerships consist of two or more people. An oral partnership is legal, but it is much wiser to have a signed legal partnership agreement.

Corporations require securing a corporate name, preparing the Articles of Incorporation, and paying all state filing fees.

CHAPTER 3

WHAT'S NEXT

A PLACE OF YOUR OWN...If you are considering your home as your place of business you must comply with the zoning laws in your community. Usually condominiums or planned communities have rules of their own about running a business. These zoning laws will stipulate what kind of business you may or may not conduct from your home.

No matter what your talent or service—you will be in <u>someone's</u> way if you are working out of your home—unless you establish your own space. Set up your workspace so it shows that you take yourself and your work very seriously. It doesn't matter where in your house you set up your office or work area—but you must train your family to respect your space and privacy, especially if you have young children.

MY PLACE...WITH SOME ADVICE... I
started working in the basement, which we use
as a part of our living area, and the mess was
always visible. Believe me this did not make
my husband very happy.

After a little friendly persuasion, I talked him
into letting me take over his work-room and we
would move his tools to another place. I
figured this room would be perfect—larger than
I needed—a nice work-bench to use for
"creating"—and it even had a door! I was so
excited! Now it seemed like I really had a
business and not just a hobby.

It didn't take me long to fill up this room!
Now I needed <u>more</u> space, so we had pull-down
stairs installed and a floor laid in our attic. I
figured if I couldn't spread out—I'd go up!

Once again I thought I had SO MUCH
room—but after 7 years I have out grown
both the room in the basement and the attic—
and I only do silk flowers as a part time
business! This crowded space problem forces

me to keep my "shop" cleaned up just so I have a place to stand and work. (Believe me there are many times when there is only standing room.)

By now I had utilized every inch of space I could, and even hung my baskets from the ceiling— this got them off the floor and still visible to pick for a project. Baskets hanging from the low basement ceiling also kept anyone taller than me out of my "space."

I found an old dresser that worked great for storing ribbon and miscellaneous supplies—and also used some old file cabinets. Garage sales are a great place to find cabinets to use for storage.

If you have an empty wall—put up peg board or wood lattice. You will be able to hang lots of "stuff."

Another mistake I made was to purchase cheap shelves—the metal kind you put together. They weren't very sturdy and I was afraid they would fall over. So after I made a little money I purchased adjustable, heavy, steel shelves. They cost a little more than I wanted to spend but they were well worth it. (The first shelves I purchased were so wobbly that I pounded nails into the walls and tied the shelves to the nails so they wouldn't fall over.)

It was amazing how many people wanted to help me get started. I had people giving me baskets, flowers, vases—all the things they thought were too good to throw away, but really didn't want or need. One lady even purchased baskets for me at a garage sale. (I gladly re-paid for them.)

I was very happy and appreciated all they gave me—no one gave me anything when I had the worm business. I <u>still</u> take anything people want to give me—(at the same time I am accepting other people's "stuff", I am trying to "tune out" my husband's objections). It all comes in handy and can save money, especially when you least expect. And now you know why I have a space problem!

I purchased large plastic tubs (with lids) for storage of seasonal items. Try to get the ones that are clear so you can see what is in them.

I was not quite that smart so I have to open them to see what is inside. I have them marked for the seasons and then when I am finished with Spring, Fall, Summer, Christmas etc. I just put all my supplies in a tub and store until the next year.

TELEPHONES...If you are working out of your home, you must make a decision as to how you will handle the phone calls. Should you install a separate line for your business? If you have a family answering machine, do you want to design a message that includes your business information? I have found that customers will leave messages on the tape and don't seem to be upset when a human does not answer—but it is better business practice to install a separate phone line for your business.

You can purchase software for your computer which will double as a fax machine and a telephone with an answering machine. Again you will have to have a separate telephone line for the computer.

MAILING ADDRESS...If you have created professional stationery, envelopes, and business Cards, it should not be a problem for you to use your home address as your business address.

Post office box addresses are a dead give away that you have a home-based office. If you don't want people to know you are using your home and need to have packages delivered then use both the P.O. Box and the street address. Add the P.O. Box number to the end of the zip code.

TEST THE WATER BEFORE YOU JUMP...Fifty percent of small businesses do not survive year two because they did not have enough capital and spread themselves too thin.

They decide to start a business, and immediately think they need a big, beautiful store. I know a successful man that started his business selling out of his car. (Don't laugh, it was clothes, not drugs.)

Don't make the mistake of thinking too big—unless you have plenty of money and don't mind loosing it, that is. You can be professional and still work out of your house. Just think of the overhead expense you are saving, and the best part—the savings goes right to the "bottom line." Isn't profit why you want your own business?

Now don't misunderstand, I think it is wonderful if you can afford to open your own store. However, before you run out and rent that building make a "pros and cons" list. List all the reasons you should have a building and the reasons that it is not a good idea. Make sure you include rent, utilities, insurance, and payroll. Payroll? Yes, remember, you will not be able to be at the store every hour, every day. Which column is bigger? That's your answer.

Consider your location. Is there competition near you? You don't want to make it too convenient for your customers to "shop around" for a better price.

RELOCATE YOUR BUSINESS... Every state has offices to explain the necessary licenses needed, loan programs, and zoning laws required for a small business.

If you are planning to relocate to another state, it would be wise to contact the state offices to find out the particulars for that state before you move your business.

CASH... Most small businesses will operate at a loss for the first year of operation. Make sure you have adequate funds and a plan "B" if "A" is a flop. Most business failures are due to lack of capital. If you are employed, try to keep your regular job during start-up. Sometimes it is really tough, but it will help the "slow months" pass by less painfully.

The best source for financial help when starting up your business is <u>yourself</u>. If you have savings that will be enough to help establish your business and also for personal emergencies—then borrow from yourself!

Friends and relatives may want to loan you the funds—but make sure you get a signed, formal document which includes the repayment and interest plan.

The Small Business Administration (SBA) will guarantee a loan (usually 90%.) With this guarantee the bank will be more willing to lend you money. Visit http://www.sba.gov.

Be careful with home equity loans—you are placing your home in jeopardy. If your business fails, you could lose your home and your business.

Also, some life insurance policies have value and you can borrow against them. Retirement plans will also let you borrow against them—however, if you quit your job, the loan must be repaid immediately or is considered as an early withdrawal and penalized.

And then there are credit cards—be careful with these. The interest rates can be extremely high.

Most of the above cash/loan ideas will require a personal guarantee. That means you must sign an agreement that states no matter what happens to your business you are liable for repayment of the loan. THINK BEFORE SIGNING ON THE DOTTED LINE.

*EMPLOYEES....*You probably won't need any employees to help you sell out of your car. And you probably won't need any to help sell out of your home—now if you've decided to go big and hire employees, congratulations!

Here are a few tips—remember you get what you pay for. Hire the best you can find— someone who will consider your business as his or hers, take your time —but don't ask the following questions during your interview (it's against the law): age or birthplace, ethnic origin or nationality, race or religion, marital status or number of children, disabilities, arrests. Thank goodness you can still ask for references. Always ask the reference, "Would you hire this person again?"

You will soon learn the responsibility of having employees is as bad if not worse than having children.

An employee will cost you approximately 2-1/2 times his or her annual wages because of all the taxes and fringes. And then there is the nightmare of "forms," paperwork, rules and regulations...

FICA Taxes
Social Security Taxes
Federal and State Unemployment Taxes
Worker's Compensation Insurance
Benefit Plan
Employee Retirement Income Security
   Act
OSHA
Federal Fair Labor Standards Act
Minimum Wage and Overtime Payments
Anti-Discrimination Laws
Immigration Laws

There is an alternative to all the headaches of employees—leasing.   Employment agencies take care of all the legal headaches and benefits for a fee and payroll. Be sure the employment agency is a member of the National Association of   Professional   Employer   Organizations (NAPEO).

How much easier could it get? At holiday season when additional help is needed all you do is call the agency. They do all the recruiting for you. The best part is if you are not satisfied with the person, you just tell the agency to send a replacement.

DON'T FORGET THE KIDS... Check your local high schools for temporary or part time help. They will be able to give you names of responsible young adults that want and need to work. If you find a group of students that need to raise money for a school project or function, you will pay no payroll taxes and declare the amount paid as a donation.

A BUSINESS PLAN... The definition of a Business Plan is a series of instructions for achieving your business goals. It is like a map to get you to the goals you have set.

All businesses need a business plan. However when you are first starting there is no past history to compare. Because of this you will have a difficult time creating a business plan for the first year. Look for Business Plan software for your computer.

Set your sales goals for the first four weeks and then try to better the dollars every week. Keep this up for the first year, pretty soon you will have some history to look back on and be able to measure your growth. Stay on top of your cash flow daily.

Your sales goals must be specific and in writing. Find ways to be different from your competitors. Do things for your customers that go way beyond the norm. Be different!

Put yourself in your customer's place. What is the first thing that turns you off when receiving a marketing phone call or a pushy sales person? It's the SELL—they are trying to sell you something, not educate you as to why you need to purchase it. Educate your customers and the rewards will be surprising. Treat everyone you meet as a potential new customer.

DEVELOP A BOARD... Gather a few of your friends and relatives together every few months and let them critique your business activities. Tell them your plans for the near future. But remember they will tell you things you don't want to hear. Grow from what they express and listen to their ideas.

RECEIPTS...<u>SAVE ALL RECEIPTS</u> they will come in handy when filing income tax. Not saving receipts is probably something of which we are all guilty. Every time you "run out" to pick something up, mark down your mileage. Eating meals while on business, any dues for organizations that are business related and any sales tax paid are deductible.

SUPPLIERS... Make friends with the wholesalers from whom you purchase your supplies. Introduce yourself and get to know them. You and your business will benefit from the friendship. It makes getting items in a "pinch" a lot easier.

I've always had problems with sales. In other words I am a real sucker for a SALE sign. If I see a bargain, I tend to over buy and then here comes the storage problem--again. Although, I <u>have</u> had the over buying pay off in certain incidents.

As time goes on and your customer base grows—you will sell things you may not like. Remember everyone's tastes are different—so don't be too hard on yourself if you create something you don't like—someone else may love it. And some of the "mistakes" you purchased or think you created may sell at a later date.

The longer you are in business the more you will receive catalogs for supplies you may need. This will also help you to see what is selling and determine what you need to order. Catalog shopping also allows you to "shop" for bargain prices and generally saves the tax.

MARKETING and CUSTOMER GROUP ...
It will take you time to determine the desires and tastes of your beginning customer group. This also makes purchasing raw materials a little more difficult.

Talk to your customers, see what they need or want and make them come first before anything or anyone else. Once you have established a relationship with them you can then strategically gear your creations and services to meet their needs. The wants, needs, and desires of a "Saks Fifth Avenue" shopper will not be the same as the "K-Mart or Wal-Mart" shopper.

The customer does not exist for your business, your business exists for the customer. THE CUSTOMER IS ALWAYS RIGHT!

CHAPTER 4

PURCHASING

WHAT DO I NEED? If you are a "crafty" person, you probably have most of what you need already. You don't need to buy all new equipment—unless you are creating in front of the public, who's going to see it? Chances are you will never be able to find a replacement that is better than that old "tool" you have been using for years.

If you plan on selling a service, you will have to evaluate what your needs will be—cleaning supplies, pet food, groceries, etc.

RAW MATERIALS...Only purchase the raw materials you need for a short period. Just as I mentioned in Chapter 2, you may change your mind about what you want to sell.

Watch for seasonal and store sales. The problem with this is you have to invest money after the season and you will have to wait a whole year to recover your money with finished products, and you will need storage space.

Try to purchase as much as you can wholesale. Check the yellow pages for wholesalers and manufacturers. Find outlet stores or factories that have on-site stores for over-runs or defects.

Keep your eyes open. Be observant as to what other businesses like yours are doing.

INSIDE INFORMATION and some advice on weeds or wild flowers... Like I said in the Introduction, my business is silk flowers and gift baskets—it may not even be close to what you plan to sell, but the experience, I feel, is worth passing along.

After I had gotten my feet wet and spent lots of money on the raw materials I <u>thought</u> I needed, I began to realize that a lot of the dried flowers and fillers I was using were right in front of my eyes—GROWING ON THE SIDE OF THE ROAD! Yee Gads! How stupid I had been!

I thought about it for a few days. I became more excited the more I thought. My husband and I took the car to a wooded area one Sunday afternoon in July, and began to pick weeds/wildflowers—we didn't know what we were doing, but we were determined to learn.

After I saw all the spiders, and who knows what other kinds of bugs that live in these weeds, I decided I should ask my husband if he would be a part of my business and be the official wild flower/weed collector.

It became very exciting to learn which weeds oops, wild flowers, would dry and be useable. Clear acrylic spray, we learned, preserved the wild flowers and kept them from falling apart.

My husband was on a mission! He would stop on his way home from his office and gather "stuff" for us to dry. After awhile we learned what was good and what didn't dry very well. Cat tails held up perfectly if sprayed with acrylic. He had become the "expert."

The farmers (from whom he had permission) got used to seeing him in the fields, and the police just slowed down and waved.

Don't pick anything from a public place or the side of a highway—this is usually illegal.

And then the "light bulb" came on again as I was searching for the "right color" for a flower arrangement someone had ordered. SPRAY PAINT! I couldn't believe I hadn't thought of this sooner. I don't worry about the "right" color any more. I make it the "right" color.

PACKAGING ... Packaging is almost as important as how and where you sell your creations. "Service" sales usually don't take a bag.

If you can use plastic bags for your crafty sales, order white—they look more professional than the colored bags. At the start, keep your eyes open, some stores use unmarked bags.

Some of these stores may be willing to sell you a few or you may be able to collect some not too "used" bags. Then if you order pressure sensitive stickers with your name, logo, etc., (which by the way is a lot cheaper than ordering printed bags) you can use these on the plastic bags. As time goes on you will be ready to order specific sizes, colors of bags, boxes, and sensitive labels.

*AND SOME OF MY EXPERIENCES WITH PACKAGING...*I started one year in advance to make 40—3 foot high flower topiary trees for table decorations for my son and daughter-in-law's wedding. They were beautiful, but I had to keep them clean and undamaged. I very meekly walked into the local dry cleaners and asked if they would sell me some plastic bags. "Sure, no problem. How many do you need?" I was elated. I purchased plain plastic (gown and suit sizes) from them. The bags slipped right over the top of the topiary trees—they were perfect.

Back to the problem of storage—I had to find a temporary home for all the topiary trees. One of the bridesmaids took several to a spare bedroom she had in her home—her 4 year old niece while visiting went into the bedroom and then came back to the kitchen to announce, "Auntie, you have a forest growing in your bedroom!"

ANOTHER EXCITING DISCOVERY... I was very frustrated with my gift baskets, they didn't look as professional as I wanted and the items inside were always falling down too far inside the basket. Then one day when I was grocery shopping there it was—the answer— the fruit baskets were wrapped in "shrink wrap." The manager of the store was kind enough to give me the name of their supplier and I was on my way. WOW, another problem solved! I felt I was really on a roll.

I contacted the company for the shrink wrap and learned they sold it in different size bags as well as rolls. Bags were perfect! Much easier to get the "loaded" basket into.

I had an old hair dryer that really wasn't as powerful as I liked for drying my hair—but it was perfect for the shrink wrap. Don't get the shrink wrap too hot or it will get a hole in it.

And now a turn table. Expensive turntables can be purchased through the shrink wrap catalog—but I was on a budget. I spotted the kitchen spice turntable and tried it out. PERFECT!

Fill the basket—place in the shrink wrap bag, tie top, and place on turn table. Turn as heating to give a uniform shrinking to the bag.

For filler in the bottom of the baskets, I purchase Easter grass (off season, when it is on sale) in different colors. It is generally easy to find and cheaper than the other materials.

WORM PACKAGING…Packaging for worms was quite a different story. First you had to harvest the worms out of their beds (beds were 8' x 3'). Using a hay fork you had to shovel some of the worm bed into "holding beds." Which, as the name says, holds the worms while you are weighing and packing them.

Sometimes a holding bed will sour for different reasons. When this happens the worms will crawl out of the bed and look for another place to live. Now, I can tell you are already getting the picture—I had the holding beds in the basement, which as I said earlier was a part of our living space. Our basement has a family room, bedroom, and bathroom. I figured they would be okay over the weekend. We were getting out-of-town company and I didn't have time to pack them.

It wasn't a good idea to let the out-of-town company have the basement bedroom and bathroom.

Yes, the beds soured, and yes the worms crawled out—they were everywhere—especially in the shower. Needless to say our company was horrified—thank goodness they were relatives. We still laugh about my brother-in-law yelling, "There are worms in the shower!"

Now back to harvesting and packing—worms are blind, deaf, and cannot live in the light (their skin will dry out).

Packaging worms was simple, after I experimented awhile. I used a desk lamp on a wooden board. I piled up a mound of worm filled dirt and slightly scrapped the top dirt off. As I scrapped off the dirt the worms would go deeper to stay out of the light—eventually no dirt—only worms. Then they had to be weighed. Generally 1,000 worms will equal a pound and they were sold by the pound.

They had to be packed in moistened peat moss inside a waxed carton that had holes for ventilation. The outside of the carton usually had some cute message saying, "Keep me in a cool place--If I get hot, I will stink!

PRICE TAGS... Small sticky labels can be bought at most discount stores or office supply stores. If you are on a tight budget, these work quite well as price tags. As you get bigger and more profitable you can order printed tags if you so desire.

If you are in a show, it is a good idea to have prices on all your displays. Also make sure you have a variety of priced items—from low to high. People will ignore your display if they think everything is too "high priced."

CHAPTER 5

ADVERTISING

SPREADING THE WORD... Of course word of mouth is by far one of the best methods of advertising. I remember as a child finding a dollar bill inside of a plastic-wrap box with the message that read: *This bill will bring more sales than thousands of dollars of advertising.* The plastic-wrap company had placed several hundred bills (all denominations) in the plastic-wrap cartons and knowing that people would tell other people—wouldn't **you** buy this brand after you heard about the money?

LET YOUR FINGERS DO THE WALKING... The yellow pages is one of the best places to advertise. The phone company wants to keep you happy and they will work with you to develop the correct ad.

When I first listed in the yellow pages I had the name of my business in bold letters and paid a monthly fee. Only to find out a year later that if I changed the print to regular type there would be no charge. Hey, doesn't every penny help? However, in the white pages, my business is listed in bold letters and that is free.

Like I said the telephone company wants to keep your business—and here's one way. I found out at a later date that the LATEST listing in the yellow pages (for each category) will get all the long distance information calls. In other words, if a person from out of town calls the information operator in my area code asking for a florist, they will get put through to me, as I am the latest listing. Sometimes your status as "latest listing" can go on for years.

Advertising in the phone book also puts you on the Internet. Your business can now be found by searching the Yellow Pages on the Internet—and that is also free.

Telephone companies are not all the same, so check with a representative to see what kind of savings you can get on your advertisement.

GETTING TO KNOW YOU...

The more you can get your name out in the public, the more you will be hired to create.

Every time you sell or give away a creation, you are advertising your talents and work.

Every time the person who purchased it tells someone else who made it, you are advertising.

Remember to put business cards or your signature on all creations.

When I quote a wedding I always include the throw bouquet as a gift to the bride. I make sure this throw-away bouquet is my best work and glue a business card to the outside of the handle. Girls who line up to catch the bride's bouquet at weddings are usually engaged or thinking (wishing) of marriage. Bingo! Perfect advertisement—plus good will with the bride as she didn't have to throw her "real" bouquet.

If I take a long-distance telephone order, I always include a picture of my creation with the invoice. Customers are so happy to see what they paid for—and it keeps them returning for more business.

We talked about purchasing sticky labels with your logo or name and address. These can be placed on things you create as well as stationery, envelopes, bags, and boxes—another form of advertising.

What about magnetic car signs? They are great exposure—make sure your sign says something about what you do as well as your name and phone number. Now comes the issue of cleanliness—what do you think when you see a filthy dirty car with a magnetic sign advertising a business? I guess it depends on the kind of business—would you hire them to clean or cook for you?

A STAR IS BORN?... Send a letter to your nearest television channel. They are always looking for someone to be interviewed and or create on their talk shows.

Call you local newspapers for coverage when opening your shop or place of business. They usually will run a picture with an article—great visibility for your business.

Radio station talk show hosts may be willing to use you for an on-air interview. Write a letter to the radio station on your business letterhead with the words PUBLIC SERVICE ANNOUNCEMENT at the top.

Double space the message, stating when your business will open, what kind of creations you are doing, where you are located and what time you are open for business. Send this out about 4 weeks in advance of your opening. Make sure you say that you are available for an on-air interview.

CHAMBER OF COMMERCE... This a very important group to consider. It is usually the backbone of a small town. Membership in this organization allows you to become acquainted with the other merchants in your community— as well as them getting to know you. There are social functions held regularly and members take turns hosting meetings at their place of business—more exposure. Some Chambers put out a newsletter which is very helpful as you will be able to see what new businesses have opened in your community. Dues paid are deductible and they are usually not too expensive.

TEAM SPIRIT... Sponsor a local sports team, and get publicity and recognition at the same time. Members of the team will frequent your business and so will their friends and relatives. If you can afford it, sponsor more than one team in order to stagger the seasons.

GIVE-AWAYS... If you have ever attended a show or display at a mall, you will see the exhibitors that give something away usually attract the most attention.

You don't have to be an exhibitor in a show to give something to your potential and current customers—but make sure it is something that they will use or keep and it also has your advertisement on it. Coffee mugs, letter openers, calendars, refrigerator magnets, and paper weights are some examples.

DEMONSTRATE...Invite people to your place of business or volunteer to go somewhere to hold a demonstration of your service or products.

For me it is simple. I just take a few flowers and make a door wreath or a small flower arrangement—then give it as a door prize. It is another way to get my name and talents known.

THE INTERNET... I won't be able to say enough in this book to describe the importance of a computer and the Internet.

Every business needs a computer—but more importantly, the computer needs to be connected to the Internet. The Internet will give you access to the world market place. For a small fee a month you can be connected and compete with any size business.

The Internet was started around 1969 to connect government and university computers together for research. At present there are over 50 million sites with each site having thousands of users. The rate of growth is 20% per month. The Internet is made up of millions of inter connected sites which allow personal computers connected to the network to have access to any information on any of the sites on the network. It is a network of computers talking to one another.

E-mail is the most popular application for the Internet. With e-mail you can communicate with customers all over the world—no long distance charges—and the messages are delivered within minutes.

Consider a web site. It is a way to reach thousands of customers. You can create an electronic storefront by advertising your products on your site. When you include your e-mail address your customers can easily place orders on line. No postage, no long distance telephone bills, and you can respond to an order immediately. Now your business can be open 24 hours a day.

CHAPTER 6

ON YOUR MARK

READY, SET, GO...Let's see, we have the idea, the name, business cards, checking account, credit card, vendor license, book keeping, a place of your own, raw materials and some packaging—I think we are on a roll!

How are we going to sell our creations and or service? That is a real problem all new and small businesses face.

The most important thing is for your work to be seen. Some gift shops will take your work on consignment. Consignment is usually 20% and higher—all this means is you have to price your creations higher to cover the extra expense.

I always preferred the shops to outright purchase my creations. You may have to sell a little bit lower, but you don't have to worry about them again after you leave. No insurance, no returning to collect your money, and no records of what you left. But, like all good things, not too many people will buy outright. They are afraid they may get stuck with a "no sale item."

If you are a "craft" person, don't underestimate the "beauty salons." More crafty items are sold in beauty shops, spas, and nail salons than at expensive shops. Women tend to spend money when they feel good about their appearance.

After you have gotten established and people know that you are in business, they will ask you for door prizes and donations. (No one ever asked for worms.) I have found this to be a "pain" but I never refuse—because I know the advertisement is good. Do your best work and don't consider it a freebee—consider it an investment which will pay off later. Make sure your name is clearly attached or you receive publicity for your donation.

SHOW AND TELL...Several times the elementary school in my neighborhood brought classes over to see my worm farm. I would show them the worms as they were feeding, the worm eggs, and the baby worms. After my speech explaining how important worms are and how they live, I would give them some eggs to take back to their classroom so they could see them hatch and grow.

I didn't need the advertisement, as I was wholesaling only, but it was a good community effort and the kids had a great time.

Even after 25 years they still call me "the worm lady."

SHOWS...Walk as many shows as you can—you will then get the feel as to what the customer base is like—are they buying expensive items or just the less costly things. What are the other people selling? Is there a lot of competition? Then narrow down which shows you think will benefit your business the most. Exhibiting in a show that strictly deals with Indian art and you are selling Victorian ceramics is probably a mistake.

Shows are usually expensive—you must rent the space and have insurance. Besides the exposure at a show there is another advantage. You can begin a mailing list. Keep some small yellow tablets with pencils around your display and ask people to sign their name and address.

Giving a door prize is always a sure way of having people sign their name and address. Have a drawing or several drawings during the show.

WHAT DO I DO WITH A MAILING LIST?...
A mailing list can be the first start of your customer data base. A customer data base has a multitude of uses. The best way to handle this is to type the collected names and addresses in your computer periodically.

This list can be used for Christmas cards, advertisements, and flyers on special sales.

If you decide to exhibit at a show, send out postcards to the people on your mailing list, offer a discount if they bring the postcard to you at the show.

"COMPETITION..." The best way to success is to ignore what the competition is doing. Too many worry so much about their competitors—they lose focus on their own vision.

The best way to learn about your competitors is to question your suppliers or if your competition is a public company, purchase stock. As a stock holder you will receive quarterly financial statements.

"MORE THAN EXPECTED..." Take care of your customer and your customer will take care of you. Give your customer an unexpected gift—just for "goodwill." A letter opener, paper weight, coffee cup all imprinted with your company name will not only create a bond between you and your customer, it will serve as advertisement.

Always exceed your customer's expectations.

Good service generally goes unnoticed, exceptional service gets noticed—but so does poor service.

CHAPTER 7

PRICING AND PAYMENTS

HOW MUCH IS TOO MUCH?...There is no stead-fast rule for setting prices. Artists tend to price their work high. Crafty people tend to set their prices too low.

People do not make decisions on a purchase strictly by price. For example, if you are in a store and see a creation that you think is the ugliest thing you have ever seen—but it is on sale for much, much less than it is worth—would you buy it? Chances are you answered "no," unless you need a gift for an undesirable relative.

As you grow in your business you will see that some things generate a much lower profit—maybe because of the amount of time it took to create—or because the raw materials were very expensive. When you get a bargain, use that to your advantage and generate a more profitable item. Don't feel obligated to pass your bargain prices on to the customer. Some of your creations will be high-profit items and those will make up for the low-profit ones. Always consider volume. If you sell 50 pieces versus 5 pieces, the volume should make your creation more profitable. Don't sell yourself short—your time is valuable—make sure you "pay yourself" when setting prices.

You can be sure of one thing—if no one ever questions your price, your prices must be too low!

CREDIT OR NO CREDIT...Everybody and their brother has a credit card and probably most of them "over use it." It may be to your advantage to take credit cards, however nothing in life is free. In addition to fees (check with your local financial institution for the percentage of charge) you must purchase a machine to swipe the card, charge slips, and a phone line to authorize payment. In my opinion, it is too expensive—but then I don't have a place that people shop. You can always try taking credit cards and if you find it is too much trouble and or too expensive, eliminate them.

CHECKS... I **do** take checks—but I don't take a check that does not have a name on it. A check with a number below 300 is also questionable. When accepting a check, write the person's driver's license number on the front of the check and ask for a phone number. Many banks will charge a fee to the person that accepted a bad check, as well as the writer of the bad check.

However, I feel checks are fairly safe. Usually a person who is interested in a beautiful creation is not out to rob you unless your creation is made of money or an illegal substance. And, this is a great way to add to your mailing list. Most people have their name and address on their checks—some have phone numbers. Make copies of all the checks you receive and "Bingo" you have additions to your customer data base. You will be surprised how this will come in handy.

THE STING... Even though I said in the previous paragraph that I feel checks are pretty safe, I did get stung once while selling worms. I took an order for 500 lbs. of worms. (Worms are sold by the pound and this amounted to 500,000 worms.) I was elated and very naive—trusting everyone. He seemed like a nice guy and we had a "deal". He would come to pick up the worms the next week.

I spent many hours harvesting and packaging these worms and by the time I had finished, I was dreaming about worms.

The customer showed up and gave me a check. I deposited the check in the bank, only to receive a telephone call a few days later that he had stopped payment on the check..

He moved to Canada and there was nothing I could do to retrieve my money. It was a good lesson for me and I wasn't quite so trusting after that.

"CASH IS KING..." Ah ha, no running to the bank to cash the checks and no fees to the credit card company.

Purchase a receipt book so you give your customers a receipt for their purchase.

A lot of crafters will offer a 10% discount for cash payments—but don't forget to get the cash customers to sign the mailing list.

"GIFT CERTIFICATES..." Now I am sure you are asking yourself—why is she talking about gift certificates in this chapter? Well I consider gift certificates "cash with an insurance policy attached."

Think about it. You have received your money up front and have not let any merchandise go. You now have the opportunity to meet a new customer (the recipient of the gift certificate) and hopefully that new customer will purchase more than his certificate is worth. Also this is a chance for free advertising for you by "word of mouth".

"PAY YOURSELF..." Don't forget to pay yourself. Set up your books so that you get a pay check or a percentage from every sale. This will also help you with pricing your goods or services.

CHAPTER 8

MORE IDEAS

"CEMETERIES"... I know you are thinking, "This woman is NUTS!" But let me tell you—the last place you think you can make money—is usually the best place.

Nobody ever thought sliced bread or individually wrapped cheese would be such a hit—what about bagged salads? That only proves that people are willing to pay for luxuries that make their lives easier.

Back to the cemeteries—having an ethnic background, I was taught it was always important, as well as even expected, to keep flowers on a loved one's grave.

Once again the "wheels" started turning. If this is so important to the elderly who cannot easily get to their loved one's grave—there must be a market there. I would start doing flowers for cemeteries and eventually my business would build by itself.

I had the idea that maybe I could set up annual contracts with families. I would change the flowers for each season. This seemed like a great idea! I didn't think about the snow in December!

I got a telephone call from an elderly lady who lived in Michigan. She needed wreaths put on three of her relatives' graves. I was excited to take the order. She explained exactly where the graves were and we should have no problem finding them.

Yes, you are getting the picture! This is the largest cemetery in our county.

I made the wreaths and my husband and I took them to the cemetery. It was a Sunday morning and I thought we would easily find the graves and be back home in about 40 minutes. The sun was shining, the ground was covered with snow, and the temperature was about 30 degrees. It was a beautiful day—until we walked and walked and still didn't find one grave. It began to get colder, the sun disappeared and the Lake Erie wind began to blow.

We went home and decided to regroup. My husband would go back on Monday and try to get in contact with the custodian of the cemetery.

Yes, this elderly lady gave me directions as to where the graves were, (one was near the creek, one was near the entrance, etc.) except she didn't tell me until my third phone call to her that she hadn't been there in over 50 years. Now can you imagine how this cemetery has changed in 50 years? The entrance wasn't even in the same place.

After many hours of searching past cemetery records and hours of walking and looking, my husband finally found the grave sites. We took pictures of the wreaths in front of the grave stones and mailed them to her with our bill.

She wrote back: "Enclosed is my check for the cemetery wreaths and with it my sincere thanks to you for the enclosed pictures.

The arrangements are all lovely and just what I wanted.

I am assuming you found the plot near the creek.

In going through old papers this week, we found the deed from 1939 when plot was purchased—too late to help you!!!"

CHAPTER 9

THE END

SOME THINGS TO THINK ABOUT...
Never, Never, Never think...
The customer isn't going to buy
The customer doesn't like it
The customer can't afford it

Have confidence in your service, product and yourself. Develop a "NEVER GIVE UP" attitude. When I thought times were rough and I was "in the dumps emotionally" I decided that my personal motto would be, "Nobody's going to break my stride!" I think I heard that song on the radio and thought I would live by it. It's probably has dumb lyrics but the concept has kept me going.

Remember that General Motors, Ford, and Chrysler didn't start at their present size. They had no customers the first day they opened their doors.

Be confident, friendly, outgoing, patient, and committed. Does this sound impossible? Remember my motto—in fact see if you can come up with one for yourself—if not, feel free to use mine.

I hate to mention this next thing, but all of us must face the truth sometime. Some of the most successful businesses and people have failed more than once. If you see that you are failing and your business is going under—fail fast. But learn something. Try, try again using what you have learned. Don't give up—only the committed will win.

CHAPTER 10

BUSINESS IDEAS

Adult Day Care
Answering Service
Auto Detailing
Baby Sitting
Baker
Balloon Decorating/Sales
Bookkeeping
Business Consultant
Candy Maker
Cartooning
Catering
Cemetery Services
Chauffeur
Child Day Care
Cleaning Services
Computer Training
Cooking
Credit Consulting

Delivery Service
Editing
Errand Service
Florist
Furniture Restoration
Garage Sales Coordinator
Gift Baskets
Gift Reminder Service
Graphic Design
House Painting
House Sitting
Interior Design
Language Translation
Medical Transcribing
Painting
Party Planner
Party Rentals
Pet Grooming
Pet Sitting
Photography

Publishing
Reading Calligraphy
Resume Writing
Reunion Planner
Sewing
Shopping Service
Sign Painting
Specialty Painting
Tutoring
Typing
Video Production
Wall Papering
Website Design
Wedding Coordinator
Window Washer
Worm Farmer
Writing